# C

## STUDENT BOOK

# Amazing English! ™

## AN INTEGRATED ESL CURRICULUM

LAMAR UNIVERSITY LIBRARY

## Michael Walker

Addison-Wesley Publishing Company

ISBN 0-201-85373-6  Softbound
3 4 5 6 7 8 9 10-BAM-99 98 97

ISBN 0-201-49145-1  Hardbound
2 3 4 5 6 7 8 9 10-BAM-00 99 98 97

# CONTENTS

# Friend to Friend

## The Weekend

## Measuring

### A New Friend Named Charlie

## LET'S PLAY SOCCER!

**A**

Is your best friend a boy or a girl?

A girl.

What's her first name?

Her first name is Rosita.

What's her last name?

Her last name is Perez.

Is she older or younger than you?

She's older.

How old is she?

She's eleven.

What do you like to do together?

We like to play soccer and we like to dance.

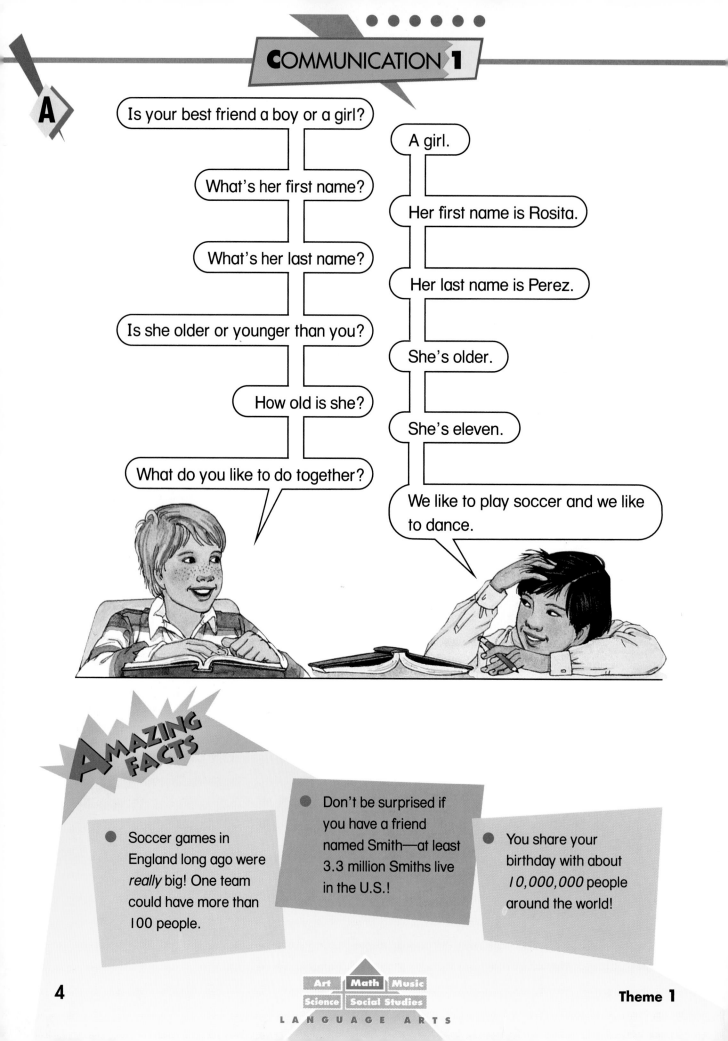

## AMAZING FACTS

- Soccer games in England long ago were *really* big! One team could have more than 100 people.

- Don't be surprised if you have a friend named Smith—at least 3.3 million Smiths live in the U.S.!

- You share your birthday with about *10,000,000* people around the world!

Art  Math  Music
Science  Social Studies
LANGUAGE ARTS

Theme **1**

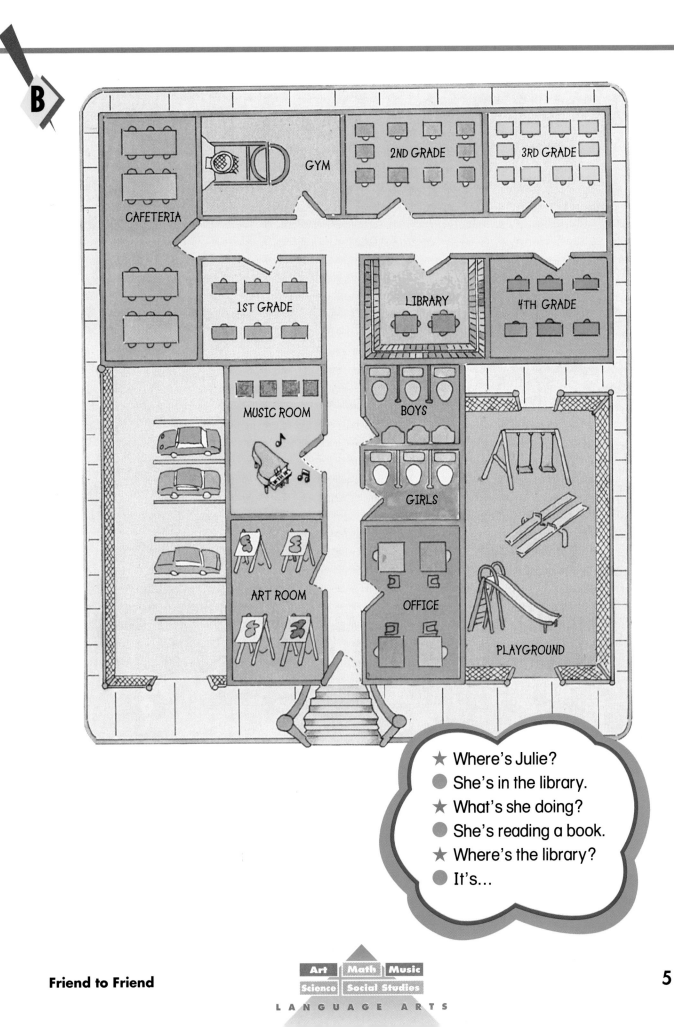

**A.** A secret code is a system of letters, numbers, or symbols to send messages. Using numbers instead of letters is the easiest code.

| a | b | c | d | e | f | g | h | i | j | k | l | m | n | o | p | q | r | s | t | u | v | w | x | y | z |
|---|---|---|---|---|---|---|---|---|---|---|---|---|---|---|---|---|---|---|---|---|---|---|---|---|---|
| 1 | 2 | 3 | 4 | 5 | 6 | 7 | 8 | 9 | 10 | 11 | 12 | 13 | 14 | 15 | 16 | 17 | 18 | 19 | 20 | 21 | 22 | 23 | 24 | 25 | 26 |

What is this message?

**13 5 5 20 - 13 5 - 1 6 20 5 18 - 19 3 8 15 15 12!**

To make the code harder, you can do it backwards:

| a | b | c | d |
|---|---|---|---|
| 26 | 25 | 24 | 23 |

Or you can start with a "key number," like 9, and add:

| a | b | c | d |
|---|---|---|---|
| 9 | 10 | 11 | 12 |

**B.** Work with a friend. Crack these codes!

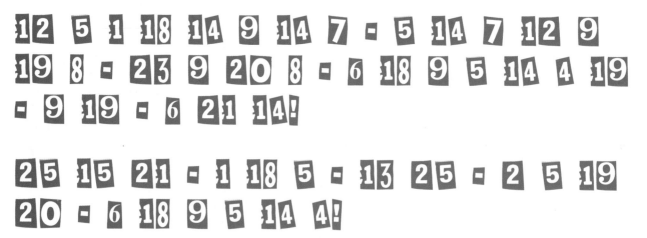

**12 5 1 18 14 9 14 7 - 5 14 7 12 9 19 8 - 23 9 20 8 - 6 18 9 5 14 4 19 - 9 19 - 6 21 14!**

**25 15 21 - 1 18 5 - 13 25 - 2 5 19 20 - 6 18 9 5 14 4!**

**C.** Work with a friend. Make a new secret code of your own. Exchange messages with other students.

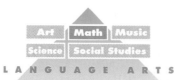

Art | Math | Music
Science | Social Studies
LANGUAGE ARTS

**Theme 1**

# The Weekend

Playing on the weekend, playing with my friends.
Playing on the weekend, hope it never ends.
Playing on the weekend, morning, noon or night—
Monday, it is gone.
Tuesday, it is gone.
Wednesday, it is gone.
Thursday, it is gone.
Friday, it is gone.
Monday, Tuesday, Wednesday, Thursday,
    Friday, they're all gone, and
It's the weekend!

Do you love the weekend? Why?
What do you do on the weekend?

**Friend to Friend**

Art | Math | Music
Science | Social Studies
LANGUAGE ARTS

7

**A**

Is your birthday in July?

What day of the week is it on this year?

No, it isn't. It's in August.

It's on Saturday.

| January | February | March | April |
| May | June | July | August |
| September | October | November | December |

| Sunday | Monday | Tuesday | Wednesday | Thursday | Friday | Saturday |
|--------|--------|---------|-----------|----------|--------|----------|
|  |  |  |  |  |  |  |

Art  Math  Music
Science  Social Studies
L A N G U A G E   A R T S

Theme **1**

# I'll Be Your Friend

Sonja Dunn

I'll be your friend
For as long as you like
I'll share all my candy
I'll lend you my bike

We'll go to the movies
We'll play in the park
I'll hold your hand tightly
When we walk in the dark

I'll hug you hard
If you ever cry
And I'll give you half
Of my Mile High Pie

Together we'll be
Together we'll be
Very best friends
Just you and me.

## AMAZING FACTS

- It takes 72 muscles to speak one word to a friend!

- Do you eat bananas and cereal for breakfast? A banana is about 75 percent water!

- Millions of Monarch butterflies fly to a special forest in Mexico every year. They come from as far away as Canada, just to be with their friends!

Art | Math | Music
Science | Social Studies
LANGUAGE ARTS

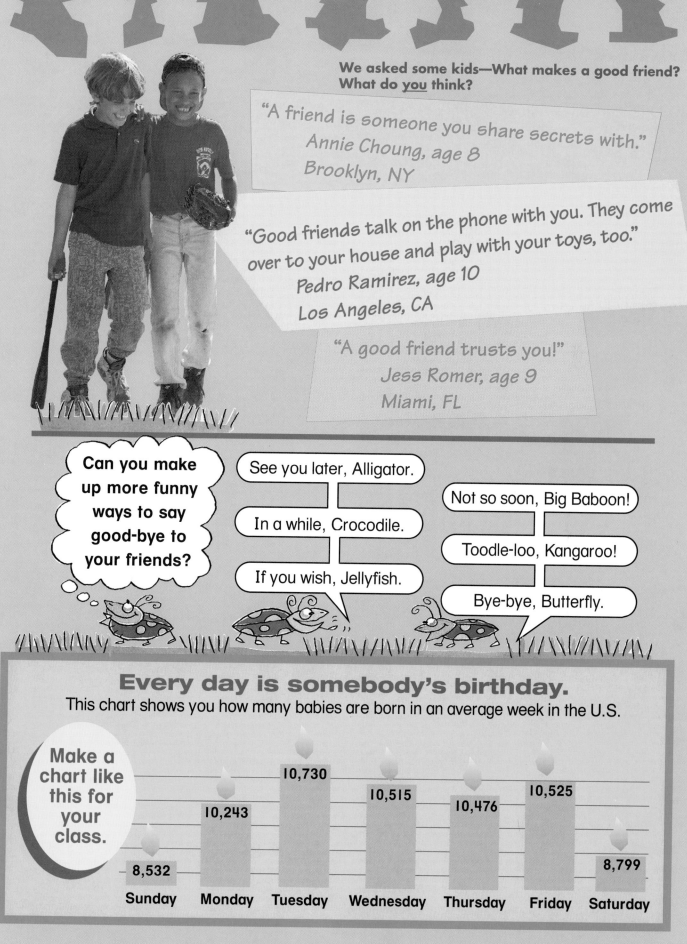

We asked some kids—What makes a good friend? What do _you_ think?

"A friend is someone you share secrets with."
Annie Choung, age 8
Brooklyn, NY

"Good friends talk on the phone with you. They come over to your house and play with your toys, too."
Pedro Ramirez, age 10
Los Angeles, CA

"A good friend trusts you!"
Jess Romer, age 9
Miami, FL

Can you make up more funny ways to say good-bye to your friends?

See you later, Alligator.

In a while, Crocodile.

If you wish, Jellyfish.

Not so soon, Big Baboon!

Toodle-loo, Kangaroo!

Bye-bye, Butterfly.

## Every day is somebody's birthday.

This chart shows you how many babies are born in an average week in the U.S.

Make a chart like this for your class.

| Sunday | Monday | Tuesday | Wednesday | Thursday | Friday | Saturday |
|--------|--------|---------|-----------|----------|--------|----------|
| 8,532 | 10,243 | 10,730 | 10,515 | 10,476 | 10,525 | 8,799 |

**Friend to Friend**

A

1. dance  2. draw  3. swim  4. read

1. games  2. vegetables  3. soccer  4. pizza

1. It's a quarter after one.
   It's one fifteen.

2. It's half past one.
   It's one-thirty.

3. It's a quarter to two.
   It's one forty-five.

Let's go to the movies on Saturday.

What time do you want to go?

How about two-thirty?

Half past two? Okay. I can take you then.

1. Sunday / 10:30

2. Friday / 3:00

3. Wednesday / 7:45

# HANDS-ON MATH

## Use a ruler.

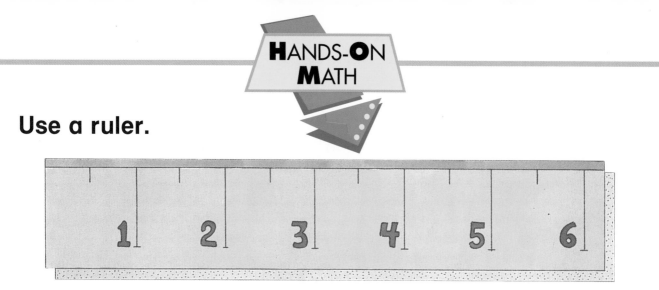

The marks on this ruler show inches.

There are 12 inches in a foot.

How long is your pencil?

How wide is your desk?

Measure around your wrist.

Cut the string.

A friend can help you.

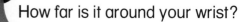

How far is it around your wrist?

Art  Math  Music
Science  Social Studies
LANGUAGE ARTS

# Make a scale.

Use your scale to weigh some things.
How heavy are they?

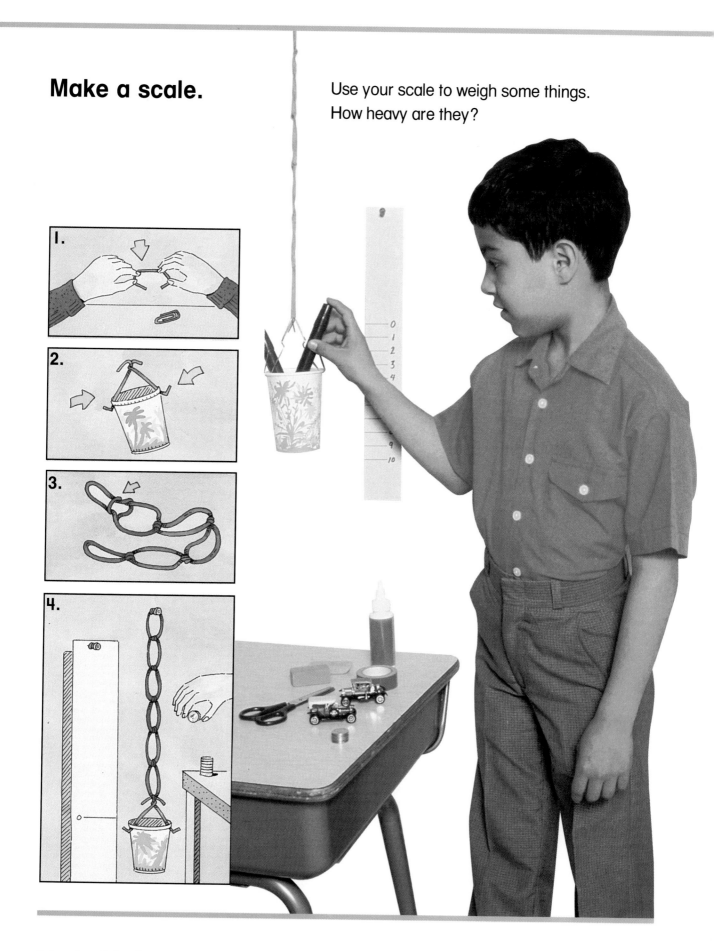

# A New Friend Named Charlie

Dear Auntie,

Guess what happened last week. A kid named Charlie picked me for his soccer team! Charlie says I play better than anybody in our grade. I can't wait for the first game next week.

I am studying very hard. My English is not very good. And the kids speak so fast. But Charlie is helping me.

Here is a photo of Charlie and me. I feel better with a new friend. But I still love you and miss you very much.

Your nephew,
Roberto

Dear Roberto,

I was so happy to hear you have a new friend. Charlie sounds like a really nice boy. I am happy that you're on a soccer team, too. Keep practicing— maybe someday you will play in the World Cup!

Don't worry so much about your English. You can do it. You're a smart boy. And now you have Charlie to help you!

Your uncle and I and all your cousins miss you. Here is a photo of all of us. Please write again soon.

Love and kisses,
Auntie Blanca

# LET'S PLAY SOCCER

**F**irst, you need two teams of 11 people. Each team tries to get the ball across the field to the opposite goal. To score a point, you must kick the ball past the goalkeeper and into the net. It's that easy! Boys and girls can run, pass, kick, and have a great time.

**Marking the ball**

**Heading the ball**

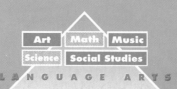

Art | Math | Music
Science | Social Studies
LANGUAGE ARTS

# SOCCER TALK—
## Words to know

**DRIBBLE**  Kick the ball along the ground while running.

**TACKLE**  Use your feet to take the ball away from an opponent.

**PASS**  Kick or nudge the ball to your team members. Remember—no hands!

**MARK**  Guard the ball and make it hard for an opponent to get it.

**FOUL**  When a player breaks a rule

**FAKE**  Pretend to kick or pass the ball—then do something different.

**Kicking the ball**

The goalie is the only player who can touch the ball with his hands.

19

# Dorothy and Her Friends

**Y**ou may know the story *The Wizard of Oz*. Here is a story about one of Dorothy's adventures. You will hear about the friends she makes.

 ## LISTEN

Listen to the beginning of the story. Then answer the questions.

1. How did Dorothy's house get far up in the sky?
   - a. A cyclone carried it up.
   - b. A giant carried it up.
   - c. A cloud carried it up.

2. What did Dorothy's house land on?
   - a. a farm
   - b. a scarecrow
   - c. the Wicked Witch of the East

3. Who might help Dorothy get back to Kansas?
   - a. Munchkins
   - b. the Wizard of Oz
   - c. the Good Witch of the North

4. What kind of road will Dorothy follow?
   - a. a highway
   - b. a red brick road
   - c. a yellow brick road

## SPEAK

Tell about what has happened in the story so far. Do you know what a scarecrow is? Do you think the scarecrow will help Dorothy? What will happen next?

Self   Holistic   Portfolio
Traditional   Performance
A S S E S S M E N T

## ▷ READ

"Good day," said the Scarecrow. "Who are you and where are you going?"

"My name is Dorothy, and I am going to the Emerald City. I'm going to ask the great Oz to send me back to Kansas."

"Where is Emerald City, and who is Oz?"

"Don't you know?"

"No, indeed," the Scarecrow answered sadly. "I don't know anything. I have no brains at all. Do you think if I go to the Emerald City with you . . . do you think Oz would give me some brains?"

"I don't know," said Dorothy. "But you may come with me if you like. I'll ask Oz to do all he can for you."

"Thank you," said the Scarecrow.

Dorothy helped the Scarecrow over the fence, and they started along the yellow brick road to the Emerald City. They had many adventures on the way. Do you know some of them?

## ▷ WRITE

Write about one adventure that Dorothy and the Scarecrow might have on the way to the Emerald City.

## ▷ THINK

Do you think the Wizard of Oz will give the Scarecrow some brains? Explain why or why not.

# AMAZING FACTS

**1** The day before Wednesday is
a. Thursday.
b. Tuesday.
c. Friday.

**2** How many people are on a soccer team?
a. twelve
b. nine
c. eleven

**3** What strange little people greeted Dorothy in the Land of Oz?
a. Witches
b. Munchkins
c. Scarecrows

**4** A secret code is a system of
a. roads.
b. lights.
c. letters.

**5** How do you score a point in soccer?
a. Run with the ball.
b. Kick the ball into the net.
c. Throw the ball.

**6** The month after August is
a. June.
b. July.
c. September.

**7** How many inches are there in a foot?
a. nine
b. twelve
c. ten

**8** What does the Scarecrow want the Wizard of Oz to give him?
a. a baseball
b. a brick
c. a brain

**9** When a player breaks a rule, it's called a
a. foul.
b. fence.
c. fake.

Self Test Prep Portfolio
Traditional Performance
A S S E S S M E N T

Theme **1**

# Families Around the World

**My Family**

**ALL ABOUT ANTS**

**Your Body**

**THE SQUEAKY DOOR**

23

A

Is your family big or small?

My family is big.

How many brothers do you have?

I have two brothers.

What are their names?

Dan and Mike.

How many sisters do you have?

I have three sisters.

What are their names?

Susan, Judy, and Ellen.

Do you have a pet?

No, I don't. But I'd like a hamster for my birthday.

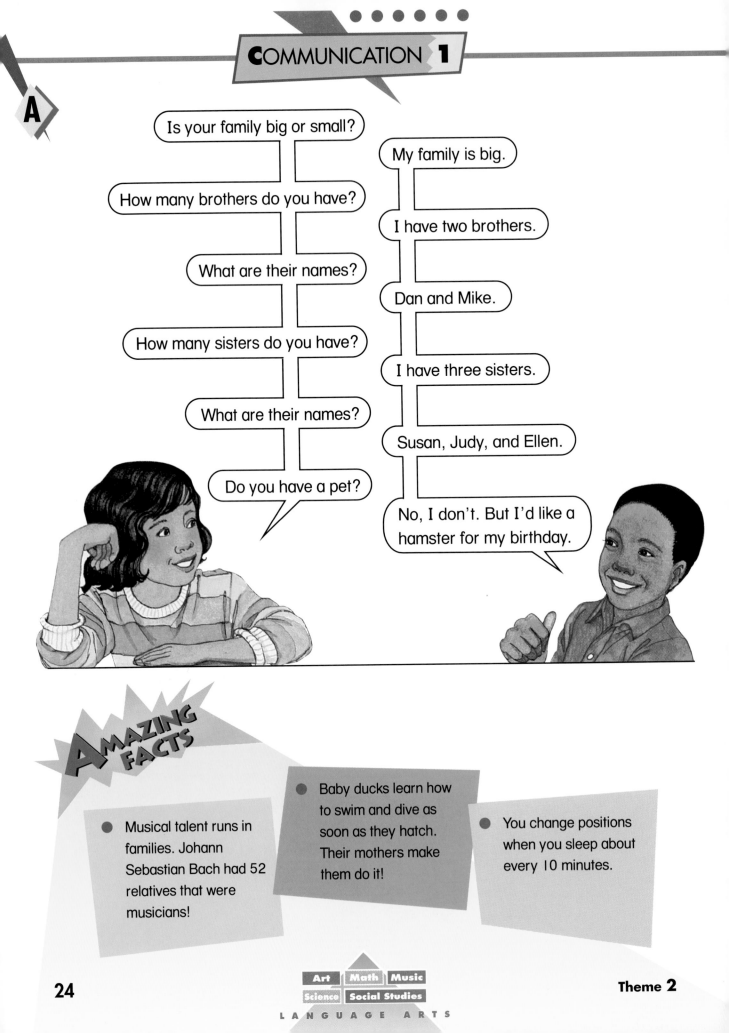

AMAZING FACTS

- Musical talent runs in families. Johann Sebastian Bach had 52 relatives that were musicians!

- Baby ducks learn how to swim and dive as soon as they hatch. Their mothers make them do it!

- You change positions when you sleep about every 10 minutes.

Art  Math  Music
Science  Social Studies

LANGUAGE ARTS

★ Where's your baby brother?
● He's in the kitchen.
★ What's he doing?
● He's eating cheese.

# Fried Bananas

Try this family recipe from Puerto Rico. An adult must be there to help you.

**YOU WILL NEED:**

- 18 guineitos niños (finger bananas), or 8 regular bananas
- 1 cup flour
- $\frac{1}{2}$ teaspoon salt
- $\frac{1}{2}$ teaspoon baking powder
- 1 cup water
- $\frac{1}{2}$ cup vegetable oil

1. Peel the bananas. Cut the finger bananas in half lengthwise. If you have regular bananas, cut them in half first. Then cut those pieces lengthwise.

2. In a bowl mix the flour, salt, baking powder, and water. Make sure the batter is smooth and not too lumpy.

3. Dip the banana pieces in the batter.

4. Heat the vegetable oil in a frying pan. Fry the banana pieces in the oil until they are golden brown.

5. Take the banana pieces out of the oil. Be careful! The oil will be very hot.

6. Put the fried bananas on paper towels to drain off the extra oil. Let them cool—then enjoy!

# My Family

I was born
in the year of the rooster
so I wake up early.
My brother was born
in the year of the monkey
so he likes to climb trees.
My father was born
in the year of the dragon
so he likes to eat spicy food
and breathe fire.
My mother was born
in the year of the sheep—
but she doesn't really
seem like one.

*Ueda Akie, age 9*

A

He is hiding. But I can see him.
She is hiding. But I can see her.

You are hiding. But I can see you.
They are hiding. But I can see them.

I am hiding. Can you see me?
We are hiding. Can you see us?

**behind**   **in front of**   **next to**   **under**   **on**   **in**

Art   Math   Music
Science   Social Studies
LANGUAGE ARTS

Theme 2

## Movie Time

**5 cents**

Does your family like to go to the movies? It can be very expensive. Long ago, theaters were called "nickelodeons." Can you guess why? Because it was only a nickel to get in!

## Just Joking

A cat and her kittens are walking down the street. Suddenly a dog jumps from behind a bush. The kittens are terrified! So the mother cat begins to bark wildly, and she scares the dog away. The cat says to her kittens, "You see how important it is to speak another language!"

## Giant Mom

The giant ocean sunfish is a record-breaking Big Mom. It can grow to about 13 feet and weigh more than 1,000 pounds. Big Mom can lay about three <u>million</u> eggs!

## AMAZING FACTS

- Are you an average kid in an average family? Then you will eat 1,500 peanut butter sandwiches by the time you're 18!

- On Mother's Day, more than 103 million people make phone calls—most of them to a mom!

# UNFRIENDLY FAMILIES

**D**ID YOU KNOW THAT ANTS LIVE IN "FAMILIES" CALLED COLONIES? The colonies can be big, with many thousands of ants. The colonies can be small, with only a dozen ants. Ant homes can be under the ground, in wood, or in high mounds.

Ants are social insects. That means they live and work together. There is a queen ant for every colony of worker ants. Some ants have wings and some don't.

Ants aren't very friendly to ants in other colonies. They make war on smaller ants. They drive the smaller ants out of their nest and steal their eggs. When the eggs hatch, the unfriendly ants make the new ants work as slaves in their colony.

Driver ants are really unfriendly. Driver ants live in parts of South America and Asia. Even the biggest and strongest animals are afraid of driver ants. These ants march in long columns, like an army, and attack anything in their way. Any animal in the ants' way will be covered with millions of bites! One way to fight off an attack is to find water and drown the driver ants.

The best way to survive driver ants is to just stay out of their way!

**A**

★ What are they eating?
● They're eating **cereal and bananas.**

1. rice

2. fish

3. meat

4. soup

5. eggs

6. beans

7. apples

8. sandwiches

9. oranges

10. peaches

11. ice cream

12. cheese

Art   Math   Music
Science   Social Studies

LANGUAGE ARTS

Theme **2**

How many brothers does she have?
How many sisters does she have?
Do they have a pet?

She has two brothers.
She has one sister.
Yes, they have a bird.

How many aunts does he have?
How many cousins does he have?
Do they have a pet?

He has three aunts.
He has four cousins.
Yes, they have a hamster.

# Your Bones

This picture shows the bones in your body.
You have three bones in each leg.
Feel the top bone in your leg.
This is the longest bone in your body.

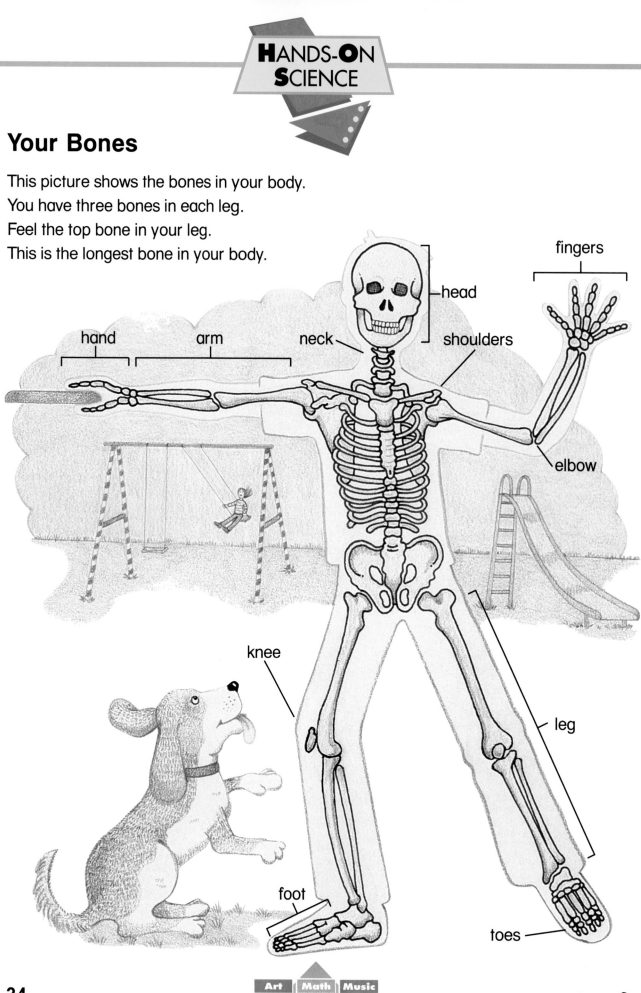

fingers

head

hand    arm    neck    shoulders

elbow

knee

leg

foot

toes

Art   Math   Music
Science   Social Studies
LANGUAGE ARTS

# Your Heart

Your heart is a muscle.
Your heart beats all day and all night.
When you move, your heart beats faster.

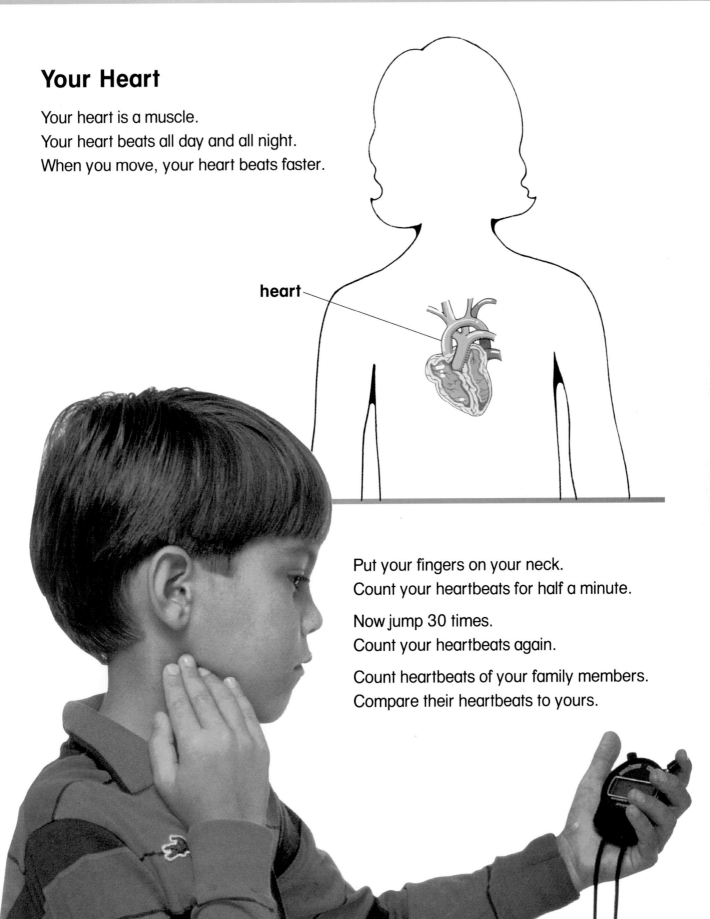

**heart**

Put your fingers on your neck.
Count your heartbeats for half a minute.

Now jump 30 times.
Count your heartbeats again.

Count heartbeats of your family members.
Compare their heartbeats to yours.

35

# THE SQUEAKY DOOR

## A PLAY FROM PUERTO RICO

**Narrator:** This is a story about a boy named Sonny. Sonny loved to visit his Grandma's house in the daytime. But he didn't like to spend the night. At night, the old house made scary noises. The door to Sonny's room made the scariest noise of all. It squeaked. Sonny was really scared of that squeaky door. Well, one night, Sonny's Grandma tucked him in bed, kissed him good night, and turned off the light. But before long, that squeaky door began to squeak.

**Door:** Squeak......squeak.

**Sonny:** Waaaah! Grandma!

**Narrator:** Sonny jumped right out of bed. Grandma came running.

**Grandma:** What to do, what to do? Sonny boy, I'll tell you what. You can sleep with the cat. Then you won't be scared, will you?

**Sonny:** No, not me!

Art  Math  Music
Science  Social Studies

LANGUAGE ARTS

**Narrator:** So Grandma tucked the cat in bed with Sonny, kissed them goodnight, and turned off the light. But before long…

**Door:** Squeak…squeak!

**Sonny:** Waaah! Grandma!

**Narrator:** That scared the cat, and they both jumped right out of bed.

**Cat:** Meow-OW!

**Narrator:** Grandma came running.

**Grandma:** What to do, what to do? Sonny boy, I'll tell you what. You can sleep with the cat AND the dog. Then you won't be scared, will you?

**Sonny:** No, not me!

**Narrator:** So Grandma tucked the dog in with Sonny and the cat, kissed them all goodnight, and turned off the light. But before long…

**Door:** Squeak...squeak!

**Sonny:** Waah! Grandma!

**Narrator:** That scared the cat and the dog, and all three jumped out of bed.

**Cat:** Meow-OW!

**Dog:** Bow-WOW!

**Narrator:** Grandma came running.

**Grandma:** What to do, what to do? Sonny boy, I'll tell you what. You can sleep with the cat, the dog, AND the rooster. Then you won't be scared, will you?

**Sonny:** No, not me!

**Narrator:** So Grandma tucked the rooster in with Sonny, the cat, and the dog, kissed them all goodnight, and turned off the light. But before long...

**Door:** Squeak....squeak!

**Sonny:** Waaah! Grandma!

**Narrator:** That scared the cat, the dog, and the rooster, and all four jumped out of bed.

**Cat:** Meow-OW!

**Dog:** Bow-WOW!

**Rooster:** Ki-ki-ri-KEE!

**Narrator:** Grandma came running.

**Grandma:** What to do, what to do? Sonny boy, I'll tell you what. You can sleep with the cat, the dog, the rooster, AND the horse. Then you won't be scared, will you?

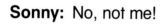

**Sonny:** No, not me!

**Narrator:** So Grandma tucked the horse in with Sonny, the cat, the dog, and the rooster, kissed them all good night, and turned off the light. But before long, **THUMP, BUMP, CRASH**! Sonny's bed fell apart, and Sonny, the cat, the dog, the rooster, and the horse fell onto the floor.

**Sonny:** Waah! Grandma!

**Cat:** Meow-OW!

**Dog:** Bow-WOW!

**Rooster:** Ki-ki-ri-KEE!

**Horse:** Neigh-HEY!

**Narrator:** Grandma came running. She saw Sonny, the cat, the dog, the rooster, the horse, and the broken bed. She got out her tool kit and nailed the bed back together. Then she noticed a little can of oil in her tool kit. Grandma smiled. She finally knew what to do.

**Grandma:** Sonny boy, I'll tell you what. Let's put oil on all the hinges of that squeaky door. Then you won't be scared, will you?

**Sonny:** No, not me!

**Narrator:** And he wasn't. Sonny fell asleep right away. So did the cat, the dog, the rooster, and the horse. And finally, so did Grandma.

**Families Around the World**

# Bambi
# and the Butterfly

● ● ● ● ● ● ● ● ● ● ● ● ●

"**B**ambi and the Butterfly" tells how Bambi lived with his mother in the forest. Listen to Bambi's questions and find out what he learned about the world.

## ▶ LISTEN

Listen to the beginning of the story. Then answer the questions.

1. How old was Bambi?
   a. five years old
   b. a few days old
   c. six months old

2. Where were Bambi and his mother going on their walk?
   a. to the meadow
   b. to the garden
   c. to the barn

3. What did Bambi think the butterfly was?
   a. a deer
   b. a flower
   c. a cat

4. What did Bambi ask the butterfly to do?
   a. to sit still
   b. to take him for a ride
   c. to play with him

## ▶ SPEAK

Tell about what has happened in the story so far. What do you think will happen next?

##  READ

"Why should I sit still?" the butterfly said. "I am a butterfly!"

"Oh, please. I want to see you up close."

"All right," said the butterfly, "but not for long."

"How beautiful you are. Like a flower!"

"Like a flower!" the butterfly cried. "I am much more beautiful than a flower."

"Oh, yes. Excuse me." said Bambi. "Of course you are. And you can fly. Flowers can't fly."

"Now I'm going," the butterfly said. He spread his wings and flew away.

## WRITE

What other things do you think Bambi saw in the meadow?
Write about them.

## THINK

Why did Bambi think the butterfly was a flower?

**EACH SQUARE =**
**5 POINTS**

**THREE IN A ROW =**
**10 BONUS POINTS**

**1** Why are ants social insects?
a. They lay eggs.
b. They live and work together.
c. They have a queen and many workers.

**2** What important food is grown in Puerto Rico?
a. grapes
b. pineapples
c. bananas

**3** What is the longest bone in your body?
a. your arm bone
b. your ankle bone
c. the top bone in your leg

**4** How did Sonny's grandma fix the squeaky door?
a. She put oil on the hinges.
b. She put curtains on the door.
c. She painted the door.

**5** The busiest holiday for the telephone company is
a. Christmas.
b. Mother's Day.
c. Thanksgiving.

**6** When does your heart beat?
a. all day
b. all night
c. all day and night

**7** Why are animals afraid of driver ants?
a. They attack anything in their way.
b. Their homes may be in wood.
c. They lay eggs.

**8** What scared Sonny at his grandma's house?
a. a squeaky bed
b. a squeaky door
c. a barking dog

**9** Ant families are called
a. colonies.
b. groups.
c. schools.

# Adventures in Space

## The Spaceship

## Space Facts

## Ice and Air

## Tip Top Adventures

**A**

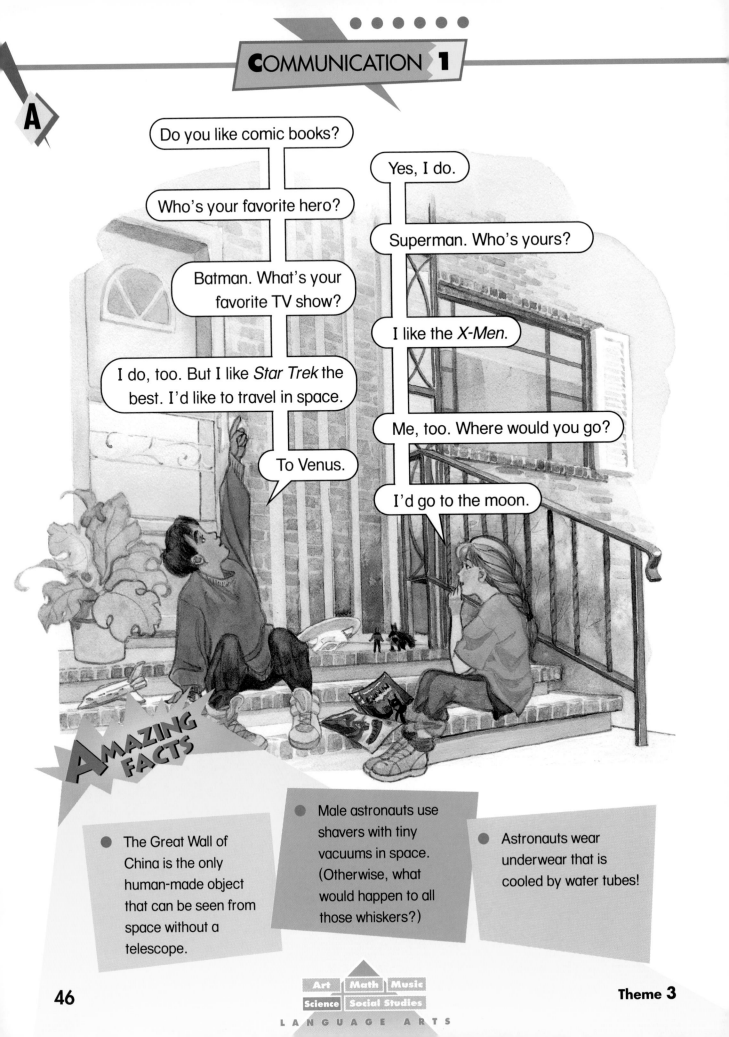

Do you like comic books?

Yes, I do.

Who's your favorite hero?

Superman. Who's yours?

Batman. What's your favorite TV show?

I like the *X-Men*.

I do, too. But I like *Star Trek* the best. I'd like to travel in space.

Me, too. Where would you go?

To Venus.

I'd go to the moon.

## AMAZING FACTS

- The Great Wall of China is the only human-made object that can be seen from space without a telescope.

- Male astronauts use shavers with tiny vacuums in space. (Otherwise, what would happen to all those whiskers?)

- Astronauts wear underwear that is cooled by water tubes!

★ Do you want to explore the moon?
● No, I don't. I'd rather explore Mars.

**Adventures in Space**

Art | Math | Music
Science | Social Studies
LANGUAGE ARTS

# Make a Rocket Launcher

1. Poke a hole in the bottle cap with the scissors. Ask an adult to help you.

2. Cut the end of the flexible straw on an angle. Put it through the bottle cap. It should fit tightly.

3. Stick a jumbo straw over the end of the flexible straw. Tape them in place.

4. Make a rocket by folding over $\frac{1}{2}$ inch of the end of the super-jumbo straw. Tape the end down.

5. Make fins to help your rocket fly straight. Tape on two or three paper fins to the super-jumbo straw.

6. Slide the super-jumbo straw over the jumbo launcher straw. Give the bottle a sharp squeeze—and you'll have LIFT OFF! Be sure you aim your rocket away from people and pets.

**YOU WILL NEED:**
- a plastic soda bottle with cap
- three different types of straws—jumbo, super-jumbo, and flexible
- pencil
- scissors
- tape
- paper

# ★ THE SPACESHIP ★

I dreamed I built a spaceship
Just big enough for me;
I flew around the planets,
To see what I could see.

I set my course for Saturn,
And zoomed around its rings;
I landed on a moonbeam,
And got some rocks and things.

I said hello to Venus,
And flashed around the sun;
I floated in my spacesuit.
It was a lot of fun.

I rested in the Milky Way,
And had myself a snack;
I waved to planet Jupiter,
And then I came right back!

*Sophie Tyler*

**A**

It is the year 2050. Mrs. Stone and her son are busy with errands.

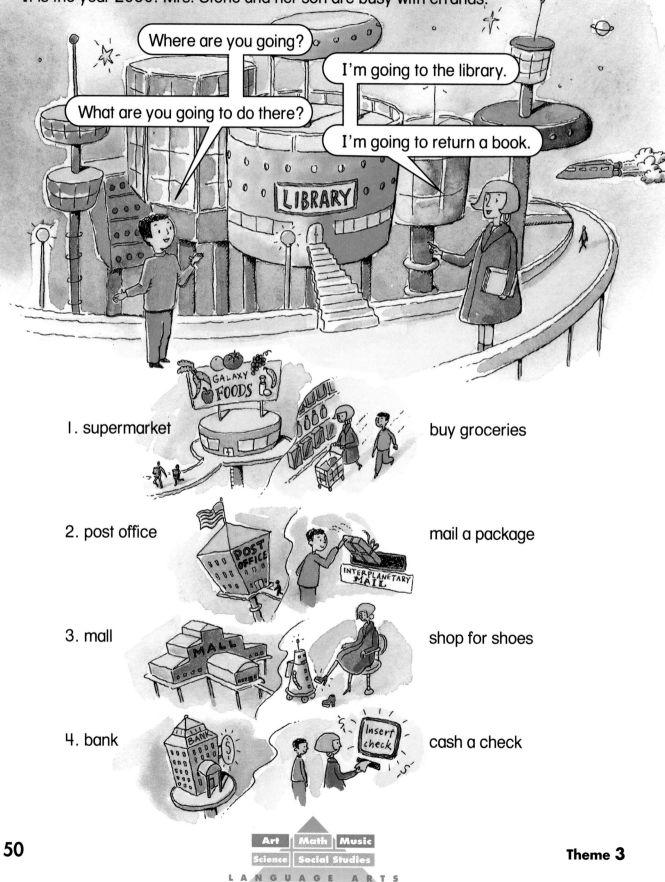

Where are you going?

I'm going to the library.

What are you going to do there?

I'm going to return a book.

1. supermarket — buy groceries

2. post office — mail a package

3. mall — shop for shoes

4. bank — cash a check

# Check This Out!

## Can You Hear Me?

There is no sound on the moon. The moon has no air, and air carries sound waves. So don't wander too far from your spaceship and get lost. No one will hear you when you call for help!

## Just for Laughs

✪ ✪ ✪ ✪ ✪ ✪ ✪ ✪ ✪ ✪ ✪ ✪

Where do astronauts park their spaceships?
¡sɹoǝʇǝɯ ƃuᴉʞɹɐd ʇⱯ

## Have you ever wished on a star at night?

Did you know that you can also wish on a star during the day? That's because the sun is really a star!

The sun is the brightest star you see because it is the star nearest the earth.

## AMAZING FACTS

● Astronauts can "grow" up to 2 inches when they travel in space. When they come back to Earth, they return to their normal height. What makes them shrink? Gravity!

● Stars look white to us, but they're not! The hottest stars are really blue, and the coolest stars are really red!

## UFO Alert!

An airplane pilot in Washington state looked up in surprise on June 24, 1947. He saw strange-looking things in the sky. He said they were moving like saucers skipping over the water. That's why we call UFOs "flying saucers"!

## Ring Around Saturn

Thousands of rings orbit Saturn. They might be made of dust and rocks or pieces of a moon that broke apart. Some chunks are as small as a button —and some are bigger than a house!

## A Big Hit!

A meteor is a chunk of rock flying through space. When a meteor hits the earth, it's called a meteorite. A huge meteorite hit the earth and exploded about 20 to 40 thousand years ago. Where did it land? Near what is now Winslow, Arizona. It blasted a hole, called a crater, about 1.2 kilometers wide and 170 meters deep.

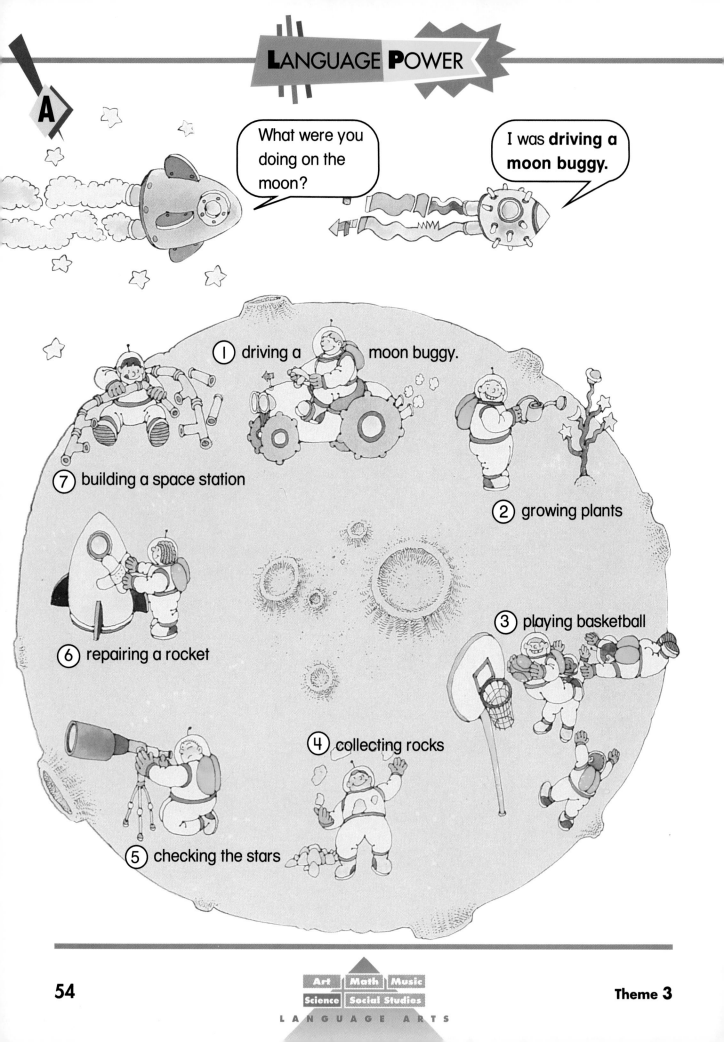

Art | Math | Music
Science | Social Studies
LANGUAGE ARTS

<u>I</u> am looking for <u>my</u> hat.

<u>You</u> are looking for <u>your</u> dog.

<u>He</u> is looking for <u>his</u> bat.

<u>She</u> is looking for <u>her</u> skate.

<u>It</u> is looking for <u>its</u> bone.

<u>We</u> are looking for <u>our</u> shoes.

<u>You</u> are looking for <u>your</u> socks.

<u>They</u> are looking for <u>their</u> sweaters.

# HANDS-ON SCIENCE

## Ice

What makes ice melt? Does ice always melt at the same speed?

1. Put an ice cube in each of two shallow dishes.

2. Place one dish in a shaded area. Place the other in a sunny area.
3. Time how long it takes each ice cube to melt.
4. Then hold an ice cube in your hand. Time how long it takes to melt.
5. Compute and compare melting times. What are your conclusions?

**56**

Art | Math | Music
Science | Social Studies
L A N G U A G E   A R T S

**Theme 3**

## Air

Air has weight. It also reacts to changes in temperature. This experiment will tell you more about air.

## Materials

- a hard-boiled egg—peeled
- a bottle with a neck slightly smaller than the egg
- a bowl filled with very cold water
- a bowl filled with very hot water

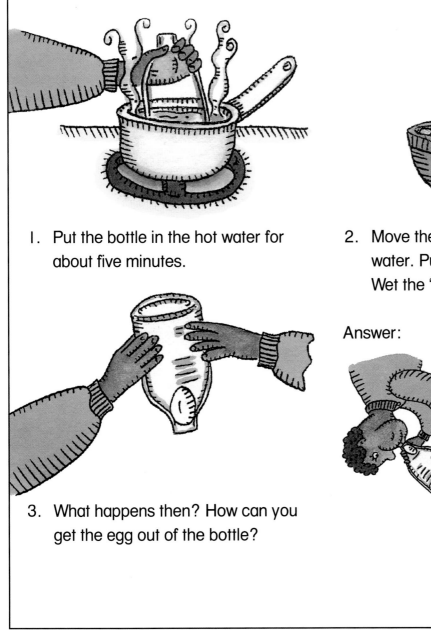

1. Put the bottle in the hot water for about five minutes.

2. Move the bottle to the bowl of ice water. Put the egg on the bottle. Wet the "seam" where they meet.

Answer:

3. What happens then? How can you get the egg out of the bottle?

It lifted the sub with its eight arms.

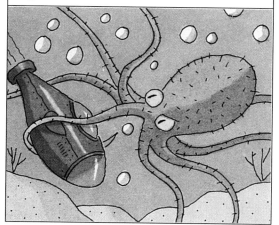

Top pushed a button. Eight boxing gloves knocked the octopus out.

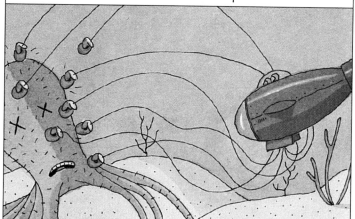

Tip pushed another button. The sub went on sonic power.

The octopus chased them through the water.

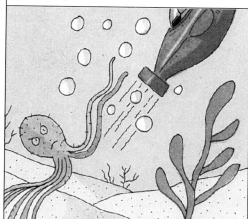

Top headed for the surface. Pop! The sub flashed into the air.

Hurry! Here comes the spaceship!

Tip grabbed onto the ladder. Top grabbed onto Tip. It was another close call.

# Tip Top Adventures

Tip and Top arrived at a new planet. It was covered by ice and snow.

It glistened like a huge snowball in space.

Tip and Top dressed in their arctic suits.

They slid down the ladder and put on their space skis.

Icicles froze on Top's nose.

Tip discovered huge footprints in the snow.

Theme **3**

# Mae Jemison, Astronaut

● ● ● ● ● ● ● ● ● ● ● ● ● ● ● ● ● ● ●

**M**ae Jemison was the first black woman astronaut. Listen to the story to find out about her amazing life and her adventures in space.

## LISTEN

Listen to the beginning of the story. Then answer the questions.

1. What dream did Mae Jemison have?
   - a. She wanted to be a dancer.
   - b. She wanted to be an astronaut.
   - c. She wanted to be a singer.

2. What helped her dream come true?
   - a. She studied hard.
   - b. She daydreamed all the time.
   - c. She drew pictures of the moon.

3. What was Mae before she became an astronaut?
   - a. a painter
   - b. a singer
   - c. a doctor

4. What did Mae like most about the Peace Corps?
   - a. She liked seeing how people live in different places.
   - b. She liked flying in an airplane.
   - c. She liked going to museums.

## SPEAK

Tell about what has happened in the story so far. What do you think will happen next?

Self  Holistic  Portfolio
Traditional  Performance
A S S E S S M E N T

## **READ**

In 1987 Mae was chosen as the first black woman to learn how to be an astronaut. She went to school for a year. Mae had to learn everything about the space shuttle. It was hard work!

At last it was time for Mae to spend eight days traveling around the earth in a space shuttle. She says she was excited, and she had a big smile on her face. While she was in space, Mae and the six other astronauts learned many new things about science and the world.

Mae enjoyed her adventure so much that she says she would like to travel to Mars some day. She likes to teach others about what she has learned. When Mae visits children, she always tells them to follow their dreams and do the best job they can.

## **WRITE**

Imagine you are in a spaceship looking out the window. Write about what you see.

## **THINK**

Why do you have to go to school for a long time to be an astronaut?

**A**MAZING
**FACTS**

**1** A dime is worth
a. five cents.
b. twenty-five cents.
c. ten cents.

**2** Why is there no sound on the moon?
a. The moon is full of dust.
b. The moon does not have air to carry sound waves.
c. The moon is too far away from the earth.

**3** What makes ice melt?
a. heat
b. frost
c. clouds

**4** Why did Tip and Top need their arctic suits?
a. Their space skis were broken.
b. The planet was covered with ice and snow.
c. They saw huge footprints in the snow.

**5** The hottest stars are really
a. red.
b. white.
c. blue.

**6** Meteors that hit the earth are called
a. craters.
b. meteorites.
c. iron.

**7** What sea creature chased Tip and Top's space submarine?
a. a giant crab
b. a whale
c. an octopus

**8** A quarter is worth
a. one dollar.
b. one cent.
c. twenty-five cents.

**9** Where do you mail a package?
a. at the post office
b. at the library
c. at the bank

# Across the USA

Houses
Trucker Buddies
Dream Catchers
MY HOME

**A**

Where were you born?

I was born in Chicago.

When did you move here?

When I was six.

What's your address now?

It's 416 Green St. Los Angeles, California.

What's your phone number?

My phone number is 465-2139.

And the area code?

It's 310.

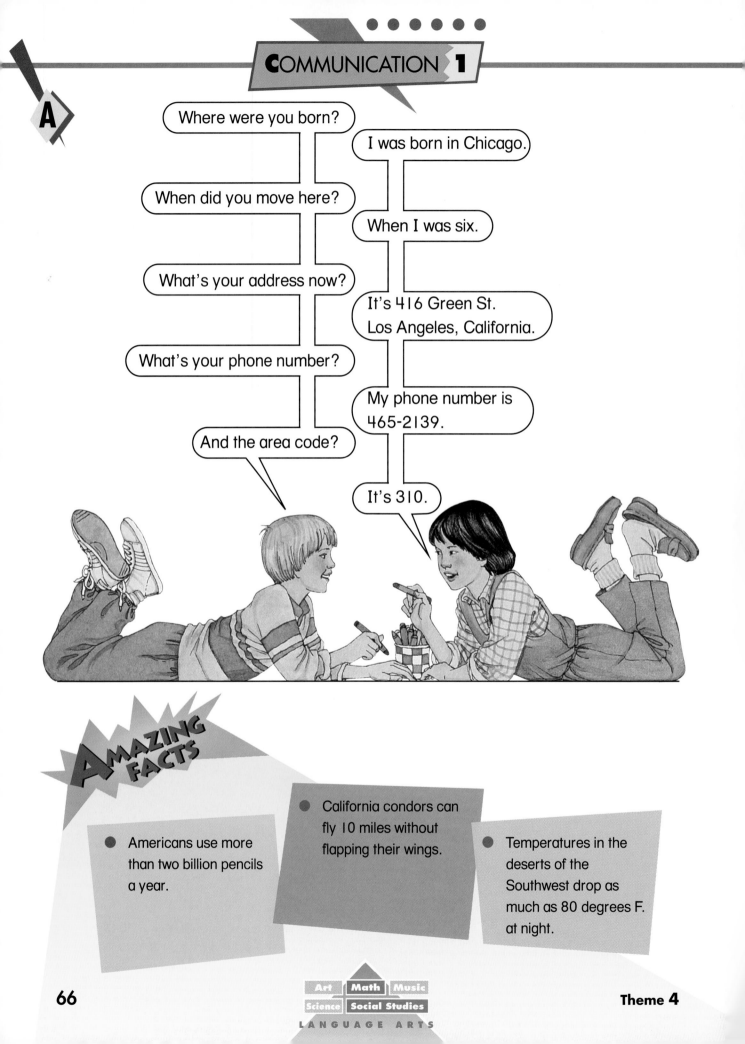

## AMAZING FACTS

- Americans use more than two billion pencils a year.

- California condors can fly 10 miles without flapping their wings.

- Temperatures in the deserts of the Southwest drop as much as 80 degrees F. at night.

Art  Math  Music
Science  Social Studies
LANGUAGE ARTS

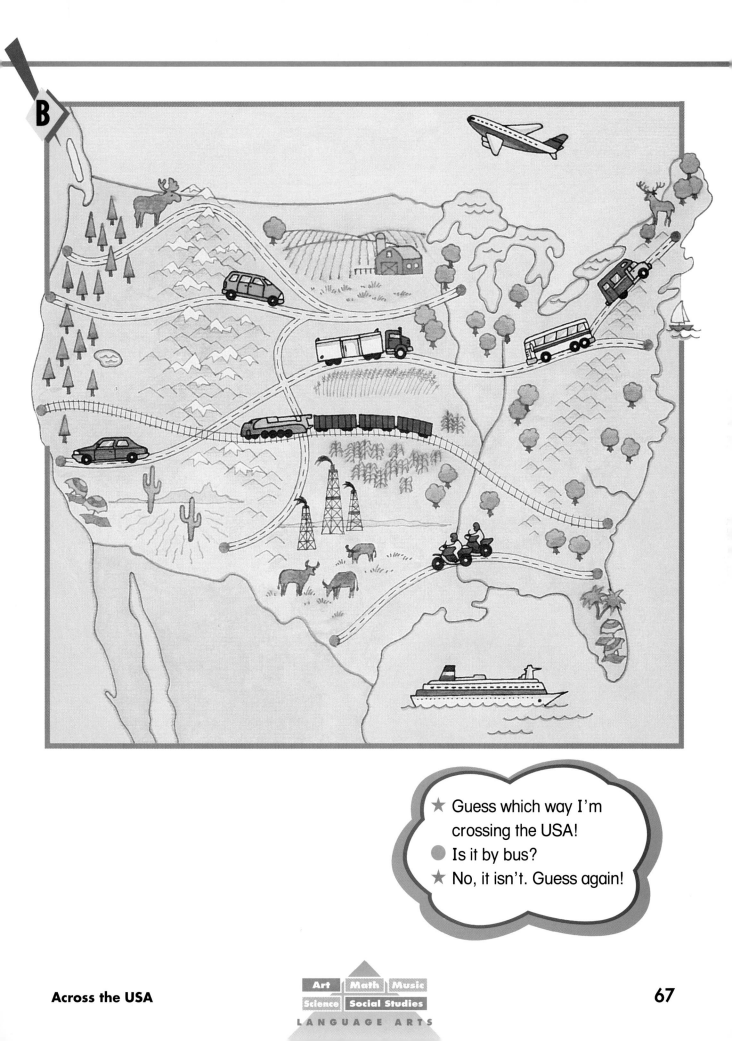

# Make Magnetic Sailboats

**YOU WILL NEED:**

- a plastic tray
- a magnet
- pins
- tape
- a ruler
- paper
- a thin sheet of foam or cork

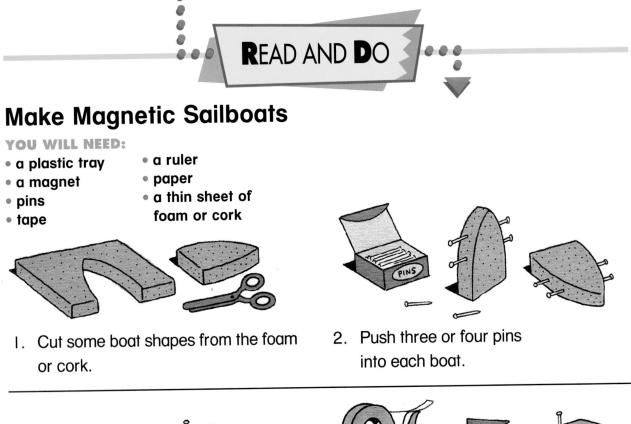

1.  Cut some boat shapes from the foam or cork.

2.  Push three or four pins into each boat.

3.  Push one pin vertically into each. This is the mast.

4.  Cut out paper sails and tape them to the masts.

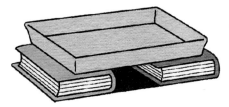 

5.  Place the tray on two boxes or piles of books with space underneath.

6.  Tape the magnet to the ruler. Pour some water into the tray. Make some islands if you like.

7.  Move the magnet under the tray. With practice, you'll be able to steer around the islands. Perhaps you can have some races with your friends.

# This Land Is Your Land

### WORDS AND MUSIC BY WOODY GUTHRIE

This land is your land,
This land is my land,
From California,
To the New York island;
From the redwood forest,
To the Gulf Stream waters;
This land was made for you and me.

A

1. She's a doctor.
   She helps sick people.

2. He's a chef.
   He cooks food.

3. He's a mail carrier.
   He delivers the mail.

4. She's a farmer.
   She grows corn.

5. She's a writer.
   She writes books.

6. He's a truck driver.
   He drives a truck.

★ What is **her** job?
● **She's** a doctor.
★ What does **she** do?
● **She** helps sick people.

Art | Math | Music
Science | Social Studies
LANGUAGE ARTS

Theme 4

**B**

1. He works in a restaurant.
   After work, he likes to play hockey.
   He has his skates and a helmet.

2. She works in a bank.
   After work, she likes to jog.
   She has her running shoes
   and a towel.

3. He works in a factory.
   After work, he likes to play baseball.
   He has his glove and a baseball.

4. She works in a gas station.
   After work, she likes to dance.
   She has her tapes and a tape
   recorder.

★ Does **he** work in a grocery store?

● No, **he** doesn't.

★ Where does **he** work?

● **He** works in a restaurant.

# HOUSES

There are houses
Made of wood,
And houses made of sticks;
There are houses
Made of mud,
And houses made of bricks.

There are houses
That are high,
And houses that are low;
There are houses
That are single,
And houses in a row.

There are houses
In the east,
And houses in the west;
There are houses
All around me—
But my house is the best!

## AMAZING FACTS

- Most Americans eat about 40 tons of food in their lifetime!

- In the USA, people own over 50 million dogs and 58 million cats!

Where do little American cows go to eat?

To the calf-eteria!

Art  Math  Music
Science  Social Studies
LANGUAGE ARTS

# Truckers and Students are
## Pen Pals!

**G**ary King is a professional truck driver from Elkhorn, Wisconsin. He is the pen pal of a fourth grade class in Williams Bay, Wisconsin.

Writing to each other is lots of fun for both Gary and the kids. So Gary organized a "Trucker Buddy" program for the whole country! This pen pal program lets students take a real-life look at the whole U.S.A. Gary says, "We tell our pen pals about places they may never get to visit themselves."

A teacher from Lake Geneva says the program is great. She says, "Our trucker Buddy sends postcards, short stories, and photographs from all over the nation. The kids love the program."

Want to join, too? Call 1-800-MY BUDDY, or write

Trucker Buddy
P.O. Box 1020
Elkhorn, WI 53121

## Mount Rushmore

This is Mount Rushmore. It's in the Black Hills of South Dakota.

Four sculptures are carved in stone on the side of the mountain. The men are four famous presidents of the United States. Do you know their names?

**A**

**B**en is late. He brushes his teeth and washes his face in a hurry. He dresses quickly. He rushes to the bus stop. He misses the bus. He chases the bus down the street. He catches the bus at the next stop. He dashes into the office, but the office is empty! Oh no! It's Saturday! Poor Ben. He wishes he was back in bed.

★ Does he get up early?
● No, he doesn't. He gets up late.

Art | Math | Music
Science | Social Studies
LANGUAGE ARTS

**Theme 4**

belong to a Pen Pal Club. It's lots of fun. My friends and I write to kids in other countries. They write back to us. We save the stamps from their letters. We collect them in a book. We go to the post office to buy special stamps for <u>our</u> letters. We like the stamps we get from our pals overseas.

Here are some stamps from our book. Do you know where they are from?

★ Do they belong to a Music Club?

● No, they don't. They belong to a Pen Pal Club.

# Chippewa Dream Catcher

The Chippewa make dream catchers from wooden hoops with webs and feathers. Bad dreams get caught in the web. Good dreams float through the web and down the feathers into the sleeper's mind.

**MATERIALS**
- a white paper plate
- 12 inches of yarn
- beads
- feathers
- masking tape, pencil, scissors

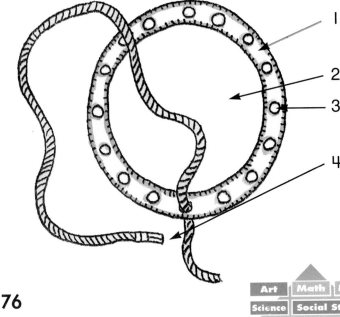

1. Draw a large ring inside the rim of the paper plate.

2. Cut out the center of the plate.

3. Punch about 16 holes around the ring.

4. Wrap masking tape around one end of the yarn. Poke the taped end through a hole and pull through, leaving about 3 inches at the end.

Art   Math   Music
Science   Social Studies
LANGUAGE ARTS

**Theme 4**

5. Begin creating the web by crisscrossing the yarn through the rest of the holes in the ring. Leave the center open.

6. Take the taped end of the yarn back to the first hole and tie it to the loose, 3-inch end.

7. Cut a piece of yarn about 8 inches long. Loop it through a hole opposite the first hole. Pass several beautiful beads up the yarn. Add a feather or two, and knot the end of the yarn.

8. Share your dream catcher with your friends. Then hang it over your bed. Sweet dreams!

# My Home

A STORY ABOUT MANUEL ARAIZA

**Excerpted from *Voices from the Fields* by S. Beth Atkin**
**Interviews and Photographs by S. Beth Atkin**

I used to live in Agua Calientes, Mexico. When I was five, my whole family came here, over the hills, across the border.

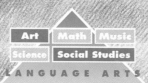

We first lived in a trailer with two rooms. Then we moved to this house. They are both smaller than our house in Mexico. That house was pink and it had two floors. Our house here is one room with a kitchen. I liked the house in Mexico better because it had bunk beds. Now I sleep with my brother, Juan, and my father in one bed. My mother and my sisters, Bertha, Fatima, Christina, and Carla, sleep in the other one.

My parents work hard in the lettuce, strawberries, raspberries, and flowers. Juan and Fatima go also, but Bertha stays home to watch my little sisters. We help my parents in the fields. I like to arrange the strawberries in the box after I pick them.

**I**'d like to live in a bigger house with gardens in back. I'd like that when I get older. I want to work in the fields and pick raspberries and take them in a truck to the store and drive my truck all over America.

# The Amazing Anasazi

**T**he Anasazi Indians made their home in the Southwest. In this story, you will hear about the way they lived long ago.

## ▶ LISTEN

Listen to the beginning of the story. Then answer the questions.

1. Where did the Anasazi Indians live?
   a. New Mexico
   b. Mesa Verde, Colorado
   c. California

2. Where did the Anasazi build their house?
   a. on the side of the mountain
   b. in a meadow
   c. by the river

3. How high was the mountain?
   a. 70 feet
   b. 200 feet
   c. 700 feet

4. What was a *kiva*?
   a. a round room
   b. a clown
   c. a wild animal

## ▶ SPEAK

Tell about what has happened in the story so far. What do you think the Anasazi planted for food? What do you think will happen next?

Self   Holistic   Portfolio
Traditional   Performance
ASSESSMENT

## ▶ READ

The Anasazi people were farmers. They grew corn, squash, and beans at the top of their mountain. Each year, when it was time to harvest these crops, they celebrated. They gathered their families together and danced. They made colorful masks to wear. Some Anasazi painted their faces to look like clowns. They made costumes that looked like eagles, wolves, and butterflies.

The Anasazi built a reservoir to hold the rain. They needed this water for the crops they planted. One year, it didn't rain. It didn't rain the next year, either. It didn't rain for twenty-four years!

The Anasazi couldn't live in Mesa Verde any longer. They moved south to find a better place. Some Anasazi went south until they came to a great river. They built a new home near the river. We now call that river the Rio Grande.

There are no Anasazi people living in the Southwest today. But the Pueblo people called the Tewa, Zuni, and Hopi live in the same area. They are descended from the Anasazi Indians of long ago.

## ▶ WRITE

Find out more about the Tewa, the Zuni, or the Hopi people. Write about what you find.

## ▶ THINK

Why did the Anasazi move?

**Across the USA**                                                                  83

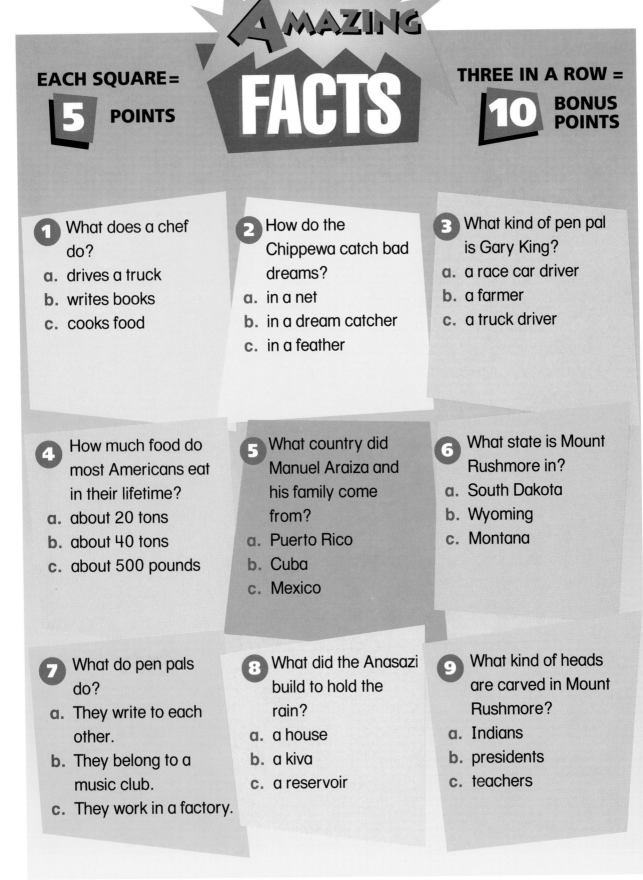

# AMAZING FACTS

**EACH SQUARE = 5 POINTS**

**THREE IN A ROW = 10 BONUS POINTS**

**1** What does a chef do?
a. drives a truck
b. writes books
c. cooks food

**2** How do the Chippewa catch bad dreams?
a. in a net
b. in a dream catcher
c. in a feather

**3** What kind of pen pal is Gary King?
a. a race car driver
b. a farmer
c. a truck driver

**4** How much food do most Americans eat in their lifetime?
a. about 20 tons
b. about 40 tons
c. about 500 pounds

**5** What country did Manuel Araiza and his family come from?
a. Puerto Rico
b. Cuba
c. Mexico

**6** What state is Mount Rushmore in?
a. South Dakota
b. Wyoming
c. Montana

**7** What do pen pals do?
a. They write to each other.
b. They belong to a music club.
c. They work in a factory.

**8** What did the Anasazi build to hold the rain?
a. a house
b. a kiva
c. a reservoir

**9** What kind of heads are carved in Mount Rushmore?
a. Indians
b. presidents
c. teachers

Self Test Prep Portfolio
Traditional Performance
ASSESSMENT

# Animals Wild and Tame

**Do the Dog Walk!**

The Chinese Calendar

**Animal Habitats** ~

Koko's Computer

**A**

What's your favorite wild animal?

Lions.

What's your favorite pet?

My dog.

What's his name?

Her name is Lady.

What's your favorite animal movie?

The Lion King.

Is there a good book about animals?

Sure. There are lots.

Well, name one!

Charlotte's Web.

**AMAZING FACTS**

● Caterpillars have more than 2,000 muscles in their bodies.

● A gorilla's favorite food is bananas. Second favorite food? Celery!

● The ostrich is the world's largest bird. Its eggs can weigh three pounds—or more!

Art   Math   Music
Science   Social Studies
LANGUAGE ARTS

**B** Yesterday, I rushed home from school. I kissed my Mom hello, and opened the refrigerator door. "What's your hurry?" my Mom asked.

"Tomorrow is the Pet Show, remember? I have to get Flash ready," I answered. Flash was waiting for me in the back yard. I washed him from head to tail. I dried him off and brushed him. I trimmed the hair around his eyes, and tied a beautiful ribbon around his neck. Flash looked great!

★ Did she rush home from the library?

● No, she didn't. She rushed home from school.

## Make a Piggy Bank

**YOU WILL NEED:**

- **four pages of newspaper**
- **paste or glue**
- **an orange**
- **four toothpaste tube tops**
- **a cork**
- **some paint**

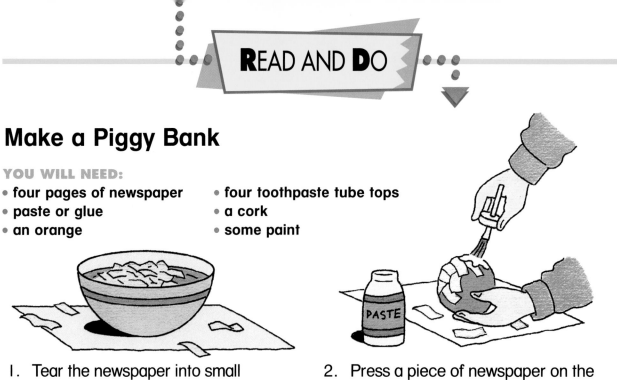

1. Tear the newspaper into small pieces. Put the pieces in a bowl of water and let them soak.

2. Press a piece of newspaper on the orange. Put paste all over it. Cover the orange with at least six layers of newspaper.

3. Put the oranges someplace warm to dry. Then cut the orange in half and take out the inside.

4. Cut a slot in one half, and then glue the two halves back together.

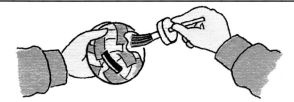

5. Cover the ball with two more layers of newspaper and paste. Let the ball dry again.

6. Glue the four toothpaste tops to the ball for legs. Glue the cork on as a nose.

7. Paint your piggy bank any way you like. And save your money!

# Do The Dog Walk

When I was a little puppy,
I'd play and play and play;
Now I am a big, big dog,
And this is what I say.

Arf, arf—do the dog talk!
Arf, arf—do the dog walk!
Arf, arf—do the dog talk!
Arf, arf—do the dog walk!

Meow, meow—do the          talk!

Quack, quack—do the          talk!

Ribbet, ribbet—do the          talk!

**A**

I dreamed I was an animal trainer in the circus. I lived a great life. I traveled across the country. I stayed in the best hotels. My fans loved me and my animals. They cheered when the lions danced. They clapped when the tigers jumped through hoops. They whistled and stamped their feet when the act was over. It was a great dream. I wonder what being an animal trainer is really like.

★ Did he dream he was a doctor?
● No, he didn't.
★ What did he dream?
● He dreamed he was an animal trainer.

Art　Math　Music
Science　Social Studies
**L A N G U A G E   A R T S**

# Check This Out!

## The Year of the Dragon—2000!

The Chinese name the years as well as days and months.
Each year is named for an animal:

| Rat 1996 2008 | Ox 1997 2009 | Tiger 1998 2010 | Hare 1999 2011 | Dragon 2000 2012 | Snake 2001 2013 |
| --- | --- | --- | --- | --- | --- |
| Horse 2002 2014 | Sheep 2003 2015 | Monkey 2004 2016 | Rooster 2005 2017 | Dog 2006 2018 | Pig 2007 2019 |

## Don't Lose That Grip!

Have you ever wondered how birds sleep? They sit up on branches. Birds have special leg muscles that help them hold on. Nothing can knock them off—not even a strong wind!

## Amazing Facts

- A bug called a cicada hears with its stomach.
- A water beetle hears with its chest.
- Crickets and grasshoppers hear with their front legs.

Art   Math   Music
Science   Social Studies
LANGUAGE ARTS

## Way Down South

Way down South where bananas grow,
A grasshopper stepped on an elephant's toe.
The elephant said, with tears in his eyes,
"Pick on somebody your own size."

**What is smarter than a talking horse?**

A spelling bee!

## Animal Talk

In English, dogs say, "arf—arf." But do dogs bark the same way in other languages? Here's how people around the world think dogs sound when they bark.

| | |
|---|---|
| Chinese: wang-wang | Italian: bow-bow |
| Japanese: wan-wan | Korean: mong-mong |

| | |
|---|---|
| English: squeak-squeak | Spanish: cui-cui |
| Japanese: chu-chu | Chinese: chee-chee |

| | |
|---|---|
| English: tweet-tweet | Chinese: ji-ji |
| Russian: chic-chiric | Japanese: peechiko-pachiko |

A

Mary traveled to Los Angeles to visit her grandmother. Mary's seeing-eye dog named Spot traveled with her. They waited for the bus at the bus station. The driver loaded Mary's bags on the bus. He collected her ticket and patted Spot on the head. "You can board first, and sit in the row behind me," the driver said. So Spot and Mary boarded the bus and waited for the rest of the passengers to get on.

The driver counted the passengers and the tickets. Then he started up the bus and said, "Here we go!" Four hours later, Mary and Spot were in Los Angeles. "Mary, Mary," shouted her grandmother. "We're right here, and so glad to see you."

★ Did she travel to Chicago?
● No, she didn't. She traveled to Los Angeles.

Art   Math   Music
Science   Social Studies

LANGUAGE ARTS

# Animal Habitats

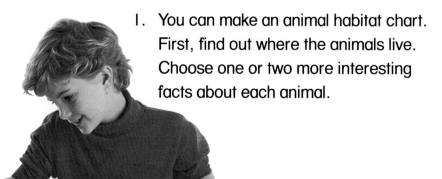

1. You can make an animal habitat chart. First, find out where the animals live. Choose one or two more interesting facts about each animal.

2. Draw your own pictures of the animals on index cards. Write the facts on the cards, too.

turtle
Some turtles live on land and some live in water.
It can hide in its shell for protection.
Its ancestors are...

panda bear
There...
They e...
Bamboo...
trees.

shark
It has thousands of sharp...
Its skin is rough like...
It can swim really f...

sea lion
It is part of the seal fam...
flippers to swi...

lion
They live in families.
Females hunt more than mal...
The male "boss" babysits th...

koala bear
They are not really bears.
They carry babies in a pouch like kangaroos.
...live in trees.

penguin
They have webbed feet and flipper-like wings.
They can't fly but they can swim really well!

kangaroo
It carries its babies in a pouch.
It can jump 30 feet at a time.

Art   Math   Music
Science   Social Studies
L A N G U A G E   A R T S

Theme 5

3. Draw and label the habitats.

4. Attach the index cards to the habitats. Choose new animals to add to the chart. You can add more habitats, too.

# Koko's Computer

love  mail  bird

**K**oko the gorilla was born in a zoo. When she was very young, she moved to The Gorilla Foundation in Woodside, California. Dr. Francine Patterson is Koko's trainer and teacher. Dr. Patterson taught Koko ASL— American Sign Language. ASL uses movements of the hands, face, and body to express words. Koko learned more than a thousand words in ASL.

Art Math Music
Science Social Studies
LANGUAGE AR

When Koko was a baby, her favorite story was "The Three Little Kittens." The three kittens had lost their mittens, and their mother was mad. Koko understood. She signed, "mad."

Now Koko is all grown up. She has her own computer! It has a voice and a special screen with pictures. Koko plays games and answers questions from her trainer. Dr. Patterson asks, "Where's the orange?" Koko touches the icon—the symbol for orange—on the computer screen. The word appears in the box at the top. A computer voice says the word. Koko can make sentences of her own. What does the sentence in the box say? Can you correct Koko's sentence?

What does Koko do when she's not working on her computer? She likes to run and climb and swing in her play yard with two other gorillas. She also loves to eat— seven times a day! Her favorite foods are apples, nuts, and corn. If you want to learn more about Koko, your teacher has her address!

*Koko, the gorilla*

**Animals Wild and Tame**

# The King of the Beasts

**L**ions live together in family groups. Listen to more facts about these big cats.

## ▷ LISTEN

Listen to the beginning of the story. Then answer the questions.

1. What is a family group of lions called?
   a. a group
   b. a pride
   c. a school

2. Which lions do most of the hunting?
   a. the full-grown males
   b. the cubs
   c. the females

3. How fast can a lion run?
   a. 60 to 70 miles an hour
   b. 40 to 50 miles an hour
   c. 90 to 100 miles an hour

4. How far can a grown lion leap?
   a. 10 feet
   b. 40 feet
   c. 60 feet

## ▷ SPEAK

Tell about what you have learned so far. How long do you think lions live? What do you think they like to eat?

Self   Holistic   Portfolio
Traditional   Performance
A S S E S S M E N T

**Theme 5**

##  READ

The lion is known as "The King of the Beasts." Lions are found in wildlife preserves in Africa. They also live in one part of India. Like humans, lions live in families. In the wild, lions live about eleven years. They live twice as long in captivity, however.

A family group, called a pride, is headed by a male lion. Other grown males may be in a pride, but only one lion is "the boss." He guards the rest of the pride and babysits the young lions.

Lions are big and strong. Male lions average over 9 feet in length and weigh about 400 pounds. Female lions average 8 feet and 300 pounds. Females have two to four babies at a time. These cubs like to wrestle and run. This strengthens them for hunting when they grow up. A lion that can't hunt will starve. A favorite meal of the lion is the wildebeest. Wildebeests are very fast and often outrun the lions. But in the end, the lions catch and kill them. That's the law of nature.

##  WRITE

Choose another wild animal and find out about it. Write about what you find.

## THINK

Why do lions live longer in captivity than they do in the wild?

**Animals Wild and Tame**      103

**1** What is the world's largest bird?
a. the eagle
b. the ostrich
c. the turkey

**2** What language does Koko know?
a. American Sign Language
b. Spanish
c. English

**3** What is a family group of lions called?
a. a school
b. a pride
c. a pod

**4** How do birds sleep sitting up?
a. They keep their eyes open.
b. They sit on low branches.
c. Special leg muscles help them.

**5** How many times a day does Koko eat?
a. three
b. ten
c. seven

**6** We borrow books in the
a. store.
b. circus.
c. library.

**7** How does Koko make sentences?
a. with her puzzles
b. with her computer
c. with her book

**8** Which is the year of the Rat?
a. 2001
b. 1996
c. 1998

**9** What was Koko's favorite story?
a. *The Wizard of Oz*
b. *Bambi*
c. "The Three Little Kittens"

# Changing Seasons

## DREAMS

### WEATHER FACTS

### Accordion Books

### THE GRATEFUL STATUES

**A**

What's your favorite season?

My favorite season is winter.

Why?

I like cold, snowy weather.

What do you do in the winter?

I go sledding and ice skating.

My favorite season is summer.

What do you do in the summer?

I go swimming and fishing.

## AMAZING FACTS

- Skywriters have to be able to read upside down and backwards. A single, mile-high letter requires 15 minutes of fancy flying.

- James Plimpton invented the first steerable rollerskate in 1863.

- The world's record for the most kites attached to a single line: 11,284!

Spring

Summer

Fall

Winter

★ What does she have to do in the spring?
● She has to dig.
★ What do they have to do in the spring?
● They have to dig and plant.

# Make Your Own Kite

**YOU WILL NEED:**
- a paper bag
- markers
- a ruler
- two 16" long sticks, about the thickness of a pencil
- tape
- a pencil
- scissors
- a roll of string

1. Cut open the paper bag and lay it flat on a table or the floor.

2. With a marker, draw the kite pattern on the bag. Use a ruler to make sure your kite has the same measurements as the one shown here.

3. Cut out the pattern. Decorate both sides with markers.

4. Lay the sticks from X to Y, as shown. Attach the sticks to the kite with tape.

5. With a pencil, punch one hole at A and one hole at B.

6. Cut a piece of string 40" long. Tie one end of the string at A, and one end of the string at B.

7. At the very center of the string, tie a small loop.

8. Tie the end of your roll of string to the loop. Hold the roll of string in your hand. Find a wind and run!

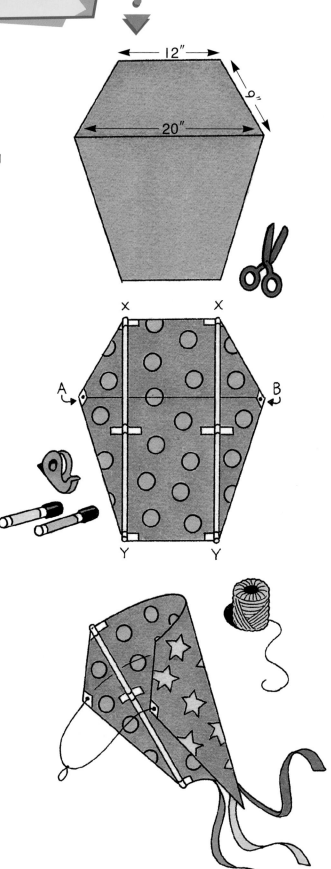

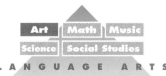

Art | Math | Music
Science | Social Studies
**L A N G U A G E   A R T S**

# Dreams

Hold fast to dreams
For if dreams die
Life is a broken-winged bird
That cannot fly.

Hold fast to dreams
For when dreams go
Life is a barren field
Frozen with snow.

*Langston Hughes*

**A**

Here's what Danny did on a sunny, summer day.

1. When did he get up? ......He got up at nine.

2. What did he eat? ......He ate some eggs.

3. What did he drink? ......He drank some juice.

4. Where did he go? ......He went to the river.

5. What did he ride? ......He rode a motorcycle.

6. What did he catch? ......He caught a fish.

# Check This Out!

## Where is one of the sunniest places in the world?

The eastern Sahara Desert in North Africa. The sun shines there almost eleven hours a day—that's more than 4,000 hours of sunshine a year!

## Where can you hear the most thunder?

In the Tropics. More than 3,000 thunderstorms happen there every night. Because of so much rain, the Tropics are the wettest region of the world, too.

**V**ictor was a weatherman. He worked for WXYZ, a television station in Alaska. Unfortunately, Victor was the worst weatherman in the world. His forecasts were always wrong. If he said it was going to rain, it was warm and sunny all day. If he forecast a sunny weekend, it was wet and windy all Saturday and Sunday. The local newspaper reported that Victor had been wrong 360 days out of 365. The television company fired him. Victor moved to California where he got a job with a new TV station.

"Why did you leave Alaska?" they asked.

"The climate did not agree with me," answered Victor.

## AMAZING FACTS

- The strongest gust of wind ever recorded blew across the top of Mt. Washington in New Hampshire in 1934—at 231 miles an hour!

- The Komodo dragon is the world's largest lizard. It can stretch out the length of a compact car!

Art | Math | Music
Science | Social Studies

LANGUAGE ARTS

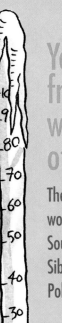

## You'd be freezing if you were at either of the two poles.

They're the coldest places in the world. Antarctica surrounds the South Pole, and Greenland and Siberia are around the North Pole.

## Here's a list of the snowiest cities in the U.S.

How does your town or city compare with these?

| Annual Snowfall in Inches | Place |
| --- | --- |
| 114.9 | Sault St. Marie, MI |
| 99.9 | Juneau, AK |
| 92.3 | Buffalo, NY |
| 77.9 | Burlington, VT |
| 71.5 | Portland, ME |
| 65.5 | Albany, NY |
| 64.3 | Concord, NH |
| 60.3 | Denver, CO |

### April Showers
Sea gull, sea gull, sitting on sand.
It's never good weather when
you're on land.

Did you know that birds don't fly out to sea when bad weather is near?

So, if you see lots of sea gulls sitting on the beach, watch out for a storm!

**Changing Seasons**

**A**

In the spring, they have to work.
She has to dig up the ground.
He has to plant the seeds.

In the summer, they
have to work.
She has to pull up the weeds.
He has to water the plants.

In the fall, they have to work.
She has to rake the leaves.
He has to sweep the walk.

In the winter they have to work.
She has to scrape off the car.
He has to shovel the walk.

After they work, they enjoy their yard.
What do you think they do?

1. go to the dentist

2. deliver papers

3. practice my piano lessons

4. watch my baby sister

5. clean my room

6. go shopping

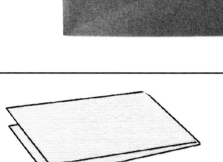

My Seasons Book

# A Four Seasons Accordion Book

The accordion book developed from the scroll. Scrolls were used in China, Japan, and Korea.

**MATERIALS**
- 2 pieces of heavy paper or cardboard ($5\frac{3}{4}$" x $4\frac{1}{2}$")
- a large piece of lightweight paper ($5\frac{1}{2}$" x 17")
- glue stick or paste
- several large pieces of scrap paper
- markers, colored pencils, or crayons
- ribbon or yarn

---

1. Fold the large, lightweight paper in half.

---

2. Fold the top half in half by bringing the edge to the fold.

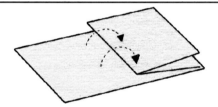

---

3. Turn the paper over and do the same to the other half. The paper is now divided into four pages, and the book will open like an accordion.

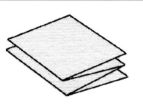

---

4. To attach the front cover, first close the pages. Slide scrap paper in between the first page and the rest.

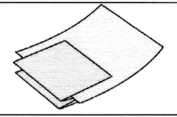

---

5. Cover the back of the first page with glue. Go over the edges and onto the scrap paper. Remove the scrap paper.

---

Art   Math   Music
Science   Social Studies
L A N G U A G E   A R T S

6. Place folded pages onto the back of the front cover. There should be an even border all around.

7. Attach the back cover to the back of the last page by repeating steps 4, 5, and 6.

8. Attach the ribbon or yarn across the middle of the back cover.

9. Write your stories about spring, summer, fall, and winter. Add drawings or photos from magazines.

10. Share your accordion book with your friends and family.

# THE GRATEFUL STATUES

## A FOLKTALE FROM JAPAN

Long ago in Japan, a poor man and his wife lived in a small village. She made straw hats. Her husband sold the hats by the roadside.

One day the man said, "It's the last day of the year. We must make some rice cakes. We must celebrate the New Year tomorrow."

"But we have no rice," said the wife. "And we have no money to buy rice. What shall we do?"

Art | Math | Music
Science | Social Studies
LANGUAGE ARTS

He felt very sad. He and his wife could not celebrate
the New Year without rice cakes. Without rice cakes,
the New Year would be filled with bad fortune.
"I will sell these five hats," said the man.
"But it is so cold outside," said the woman. "Don't go."

But the man went out to try to sell the hats. It was very cold. No one was out on the road. Everybody was home, making rice cakes. It started to snow. The old man decided to return home.

He came to six statues. They were statues of Jizo, the protector of children. The man thought, "The statues must be cold, even though they are made of stone."

He gave each statue a hat. He gave the sixth statue his own hat. The man was almost frozen when he got home.

He told his wife the bad news. "No one was out on the road. I gave the hats to the statues of Jizo. I gave away my hat, too."

"Don't feel so sad," his wife said. "Let's just go to bed. At least we can keep warm there."

While the cold couple slept, something magical
happened. A song floated out of the woods.

A kind, good man,
Poor and old,
Gave us hats to save us
From the cold.

That kindness we
Will now repay,
And give him rice cakes
On New Year's Day.

What a surprise the old couple had in the morning!
Outside their door, they found two huge rice cakes.
They were the freshest, richest rice cakes they had
ever seen. Now they could celebrate the New Year.
And the year would be filled with happiness and good
fortune.

And in the distance, you could see six statues. They
were walking back to the snowy woods, protected by
their straw hats.

# Why the Sky Is Far Away

● ● ● ● ● ● ● ● ●

**T**his folktale from Africa tells how the sky was once close to the earth. You will find out why the sky is now far away.

## ▶ LISTEN

Listen to the beginning of the story. Then answer the questions.

1. What did the people eat?
   a. They ate delicious pieces of the sky.
   b. They ate food from the forest.
   c. They ate roasted bananas.

2. What did some people do with extra pieces of the sky?
   a. They put them on the walls.
   b. They threw them into the garbage.
   c. They made clothing out of them.

3. How did the sky feel when people wasted its pieces?
   a. delicious
   b. angry
   c. sad

4. How did people stop wasting pieces of the sky?
   a. They hunted instead.
   b. They made beautiful shapes.
   c. They were careful about how much they took.

## ▶ SPEAK

Tell about what has happened in the story so far. What do you think Adami will do with the pieces of sky?

## ▶ READ

"I can't," Adami's wife said. "I'm too full."

Adami asked all his children to help him eat the delicious pieces of sky, but the children were already stuffed. They couldn't eat one bite. So Adami decided to try to hide the pieces at the bottom of the garbage pile.

Suddenly the sky became angry and the clouds turned black. "You have wasted my gift of food again," yelled the sky. "This time I will go away so you cannot waste me anymore."

All the people cried, "What will we eat? We might starve!"

The sky said, "You will have to learn how to plant crops in the ground and hunt in the forests. If you work hard, you may learn not to waste the gifts of nature."

Everyone watched as the sky sailed away. From that time on, they worked hard to grow their food and cook their meals. They always tried to remember not to waste the gifts of nature.

High above them, out of reach, lived the sky. It was far away and very blue, just as it is today.

## ▶ WRITE

What is another gift of nature? Write about how you use it.

## ▶ THINK

Why is it important not to waste the gifts of nature?

# AMAZING FACTS

**EACH SQUARE =**
**5 POINTS**

**THREE IN A ROW =**
**10 BONUS POINTS**

**1** When don't sea gulls fly out to sea?
a. when the weather is bad
b. when they are hungry
c. when people are swimming

**2** Where did the poor man and his wife live?
a. Juneau
b. Japan
c. China

**3** Name one thing you have to do in the fall.
a. rake leaves
b. plant seeds
c. shovel the walk

**4** Which is the snowiest place?
a. Denver, CO
b. Juneau, AK
c. Portland, ME

**5** What did the poor man and woman celebrate?
a. the woman's birthday
b. summer
c. the New Year

**6** The accordion book developed from
a. a stone tablet.
b. colored pencils.
c. the scroll.

**7** What can you do in the winter?
a. go sledding and ice skating
b. plant flowers
c. go swimming and sailing

**8** What did the poor man try to sell?
a. hats
b. rice cakes
c. statues

**9** The strongest gust of wind was recorded at
a. 231 miles an hour.
b. 1,934 miles an hour.
c. 300 miles an hour.

Self  Test Prep  Portfolio
Traditional  Performance
A S S E S S M E N T

# INDEX

## A Publication of the World Language Division

**Director of Product Development:** Judith M. Bittinger
**Executive Editor:** Elinor Chamas
**Editorial Development:** Kathleen M. Smith
**Text and Cover Design:** Taurins Design Associates
**Art Direction and Production:** Taurins Design Associates
**Production and Manufacturing:** James W. Gibbons

**Cover Art:** John Sandford

**Illustrators:** Teresa Anderko 16,17; Ellen Appleby 90; Susan Avishai 107; Karen Bell 7, 110; Lee Lee Brazeal 78; Jane Chambless 42, 43; Design Five 5; Nancy Didion 9, 36, 37; Annie Gusman 27, 72, 93, 124; Franklin Hammond 57, 76-77, 90; Ann Iosa 30, 74; Laurie Jordan 20, 21; Joy Keenan 3, 8 top, 12, 13, 46, 47, 106; Susan Lexa 33, 70, 71, 75, 107, 114; Karen Loccisano 4, 24, 66, 86, 91; Steven Mach 50, 51 top; Sue Miller 10, 94; Cyd Moore 109; Cheryl Kirk Noll 25, 29 top; Deborah Pinkney 32, 67, 69; Alice Preistley 78-81; Chris Reed 26, 48, 68, 108, 116-117; John Sandford 36-41, 54; Jackie Snider 8 bottom, 11, 29 bottom, 30, 51 bottom, 52, 53, 91 bottom, 92, 93, 111, 112, 113; Debbie Tilley 87, 95; Kurt Vargo 58, 59, 60, 61; Ulises Wensell 118-123; Jane Yamada 89.

**Photographers:** Craig Aurness, Woodfin Camp 82; Robert Caputo, Photo Researchers 59; The Gorilla Foundation 98-101; Scott Halleran 18 right, 19 bottom; Todd T. Hoffman 16; Richard Hutchings 3, 11, 17, 56-57, 76-77, 96-97, 116-117; Renee Lynn, Photo Researchers 65; Lawrence Migdale, Photo Researchers 105; Tony Morales 18 left, 19 top; NASA 45, 62; N.Y. Zoological Society 58; John Running, Black Star 53; Erika Stone 23; Trucker Buddy International 73 top; USD Interior 73 bottom; K.G. Vock, Photo Researchers 31.

**Acknowledgements:** Page 10, "I'll Be Your Friend," *from Primary Rhymerry* Copyright © by Sonja Dunn. Reprinted with permission Pembroke Publishers Limited, 538 Hood Road, Markham, Ontario L3R 3K9, Canada. Pages 42-43, "Bambi and the Butterfly," Adapted from *Bambi* by Felix Salten, Copyright © 1928, 1956 by Simon & Schuster, Inc. Translated by Whittaker Chambers. Reprinted by permission of Simon & Schuster, Inc., Jonathan Cape Ltd. and the executors of the Felix Salten estate. Page 69, "This Land Is Your Land," Words and music by Woody Guthrie, TRO—© 1956 (renewed 1984), 1958 and 1970 Ludlow Music Inc. New York, New York. All rights reserved including public performance for profit. Used by permission. Pages 78-81, "My Home," from *Voices from The Fields* by S. Beth Atkin. Interview text and photographs Copyright © 1993 by S. Beth Atkin. By permission of Little, Brown and Company, and the William Morris Agency, Inc. on behalf of the author. Page 109, "Dreams," from *The Dream Keeper and Other Poems*, by Langston Hughes. Copyright © 1932 by Alfred A. Knopf, Inc. and renewed 1960 by Langston Hughes. Reprinted by permission of Alfred A. Knopf, Inc. Pages 116-117, "A Four Seasons Accordion Book," from *Multicultural Books To Make And Share* by Susan Gaylord. Copyright © 1993 by Scholastic Inc. Reprinted by permission.